W9-BGK-858

Instant Learning Manipulatives for Group Lessons

By Valerie Williams and Tina Cohen

SCHOLASTIC
PROFESSIONAL BOOKS

New York • Toronto • London • Auckland • Sydney
Mexico City • New Delhi • Hong Kong • Buenos Aires

Acknowledgments

Grateful acknowledgments to the
Scholastic staff for the pleasure of working with
them a second time. We are fortunate to work
with a very dedicated and creative faculty at the E.M. Baker
School in Great Neck, New York, who daily provide
much motivation and inspiration.

To the other halves, Fido and Sam, who make life easier
and to Scott who always cares.
—V.W.

To my staunchest supporters, Aaron and Ilene,
and to my best friend and husband, Gene.
—T.C.

Cover art design by Gerard Fuchs

Interior illustrations by Rusty Fletcher

Interior design by Sydney Wright

Edited by Arianne Weber

ISBN: 0-439-30958-1
Copyright © 2002 by Valerie Williams and Tina Cohen

Contents

Introduction

At one time or another, all teachers ask themselves these questions as they are teaching a lesson: Who is answering my questions? What are the other children doing and thinking? When all hands are raised, whom do I call on? What do I do about the children who rarely participate? The purpose of the teaching aides in this book is to not only help you answer these questions, but to facilitate student participation by providing a variety of tools for indicating responses, thoughts, and opinions.

Using Learning Manipulatives

Today's classrooms require teachers to accommodate a growing variety of learning styles, signaling a need for a new way to encourage and manage student participation. Learning manipulatives are interesting and interactive tools which promote active involvement during lessons. Children will not only enjoy using them to respond to your questions and give opinions, but they will take pleasure in making the tools their own. Each manipulative comes with reproducible patterns, a list of necessary construction materials, easy directions for assembly, and suggestions for use. Use them in all areas of the curriculum to:

Engage the entire class during lessons or discussions.
Do some of your students get frustrated and distracted while waiting to be called upon to respond? The tools in this book give all children the opportunity to respond simultaneously, keeping them interested and involved.

Assess the reaction of the class while a chosen student performs a task.
Do you wish you had a way to quickly check the opinions or reactions of the entire class at one time? While one child is responding to a question, you can quickly scan the class to determine whether they agree or disagree.

Encourage hesitant students to get involved.
Have you tried to encourage certain students who seem uninterested in participating? Often children know an answer but are reluctant to participate verbally. After using these manipulatives, they may gradually gain the confidence to express themselves verbally.

Enliven classroom routines.
Are you ready to add some spice to daily routines and transition times? Make these events more meaningful (and fun!) learning experiences by having children use the manipulatives to respond to questions about calendar, clean up, and dismissal.

Using the manipulatives will help transform your classroom into an efficient *think tank*, where every student is motivated to share ideas and get involved!

How the Manipulatives are Organized

We have divided the manipulatives into two groups: those that allow students to choose between two responses, and those that allow students to indicate a range of responses. The groups are as follows:

Choose between two responses:	Indicate a range of responses:
Arrow Indicator	Punctuation Pyramid
Thumbs Up!	Dialogue Bubble
True-or-False Face	Number Spreader
Head Band	Letter Spreader
Puppet Person	Response Cube
Bright Idea!	Turn-and-Learn Wheel
Thought Tube	Pick a Number
Word Slide	Compass
	Behind the Door
	Wheel of Choice
	Time for Learning
	Finger Poke
	Blabber Mouth
	Opinion Meter

The structure of your lessons will dictate which tool to use. For example, you might choose the *Opinion Meter* to determine your students' favorite book, while *Thumbs Up!* might be perfect with a math lesson, where students must assess whether an answer is right or wrong.

Creating and Maintaining the Learning Manipulatives

Before you get started, here are some suggestions:

1. We have provided generic, as well as formatted, patterns to allow for flexibility and creativity. Use whichever pattern suits your purpose.

2. Whenever possible, duplicate patterns on cardstock and laminate them for durability.

3. Prepare tools in advance so that they are ready for immediate use.

4. Keep the completed manipulatives in an accessible classroom container, and encourage children to incorporate them into their independent choice/center time.

We hope these tools become an important addition to your classroom, allowing you to make the most of your group lesson time.

Arrow Indicator

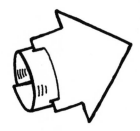

Materials

* Arrow and arrow-base patterns
* Scissors
* Glue or stapler

★ TEACHING TIP ★

Use the Arrow Indicator for lessons that require agree/disagree, higher/lower, and true/false answers

▷ Directions

1. Duplicate the pattern for the arrow and arrow base on card stock.

2. Cut out the arrow and arrow base.

3. Cut slits along the dotted lines as indicated on the base. Adjust the depth of the slits as needed.

4. Overlap the ends of the base and glue or staple them together in order to create a circle.

5. Insert the arrow into the slits on the base.

✳ Using the Arrow Indicator

Throughout the year, you might use a variety of graphs to enrich and support curriculum areas. Because it is important for students to learn how to record information on graphs as well as develop graph-reading skills, the Arrow Indicator can be a useful tool in your instruction. Upon completion of a graph, have students evaluate the most critical data. For example, a graph comparing the amounts of two things might require students to make *more than/less than* decisions. Students would show their answers to your questions by positioning their arrow tool. The arrow pointing up would show a response of *more than*, and the arrow pointing down would show a response of *less than*. A response of *equal to* would require students to position the arrow on its side.

✦ Other Suggested Uses

◆ **Science** Use this learning manipulative during a discussion of daily temperature and weather patterns. For example, you might say: *Yesterday the temperature was _____. Today the temperature is _____. Is the temperature today higher or lower?*

◆ **Math** Students need to develop an understanding of time passage. Pose this question: *Does it take more or less time to _____ or _____? Encourage students to explain their answers.*

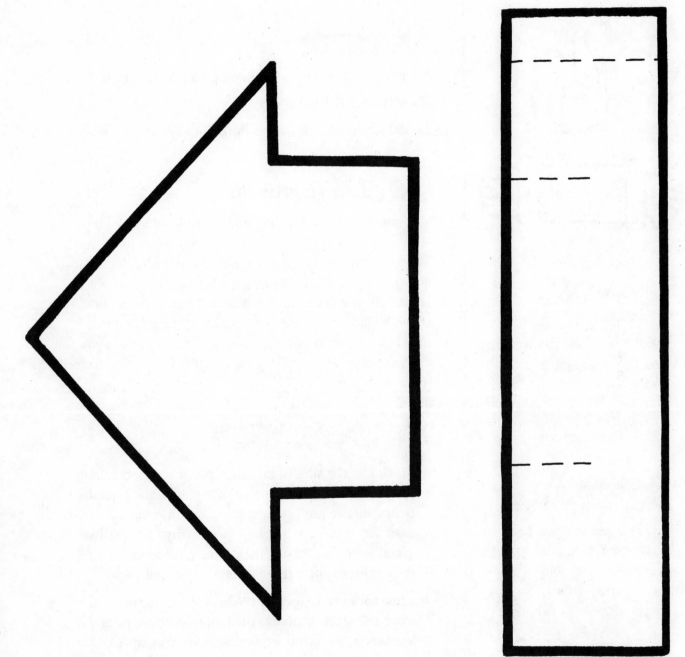

Thumbs Up!

TEACHING TIP

Encourage students to color the hand patterns to make them their own. They can add rings, bracelets, or even the sleeve of a favorite shirt.

Directions

1. Reproduce either of the hand patterns on card stock.

2. Cut out the hand pattern.

3. Attach hand or finger sections with paper fasteners.

Using Thumbs Up!

You might use this learning manipulative to access your students' knowledge of a particular topic prior to instruction. Make a list of the facts to be covered during instruction, and then ask students to decide whether they are right or wrong. As you examine each fact, instruct students to show a *thumbs up* if the fact is right, or a *thumbs down* if they believe it to be wrong. Based on the responses, you can evaluate students' knowledge and adjust instruction to meet their needs.

Other Suggested Uses

◆ **Math** Use the single-hand manipulative as a graphing tool. Considering the topic of the graph, ask a question that would require students to show an opinion. For example, if you are graphing how many students like pizza, instead of raising their hands, students would respond showing either *thumbs up* or *thumbs down*.

◆ **Classroom management** When you introduce a new story, ask students to use the tool to indicate prior knowledge of the book. As you read, students can respond to character actions by showing *thumbs up* or *thumbs down*.

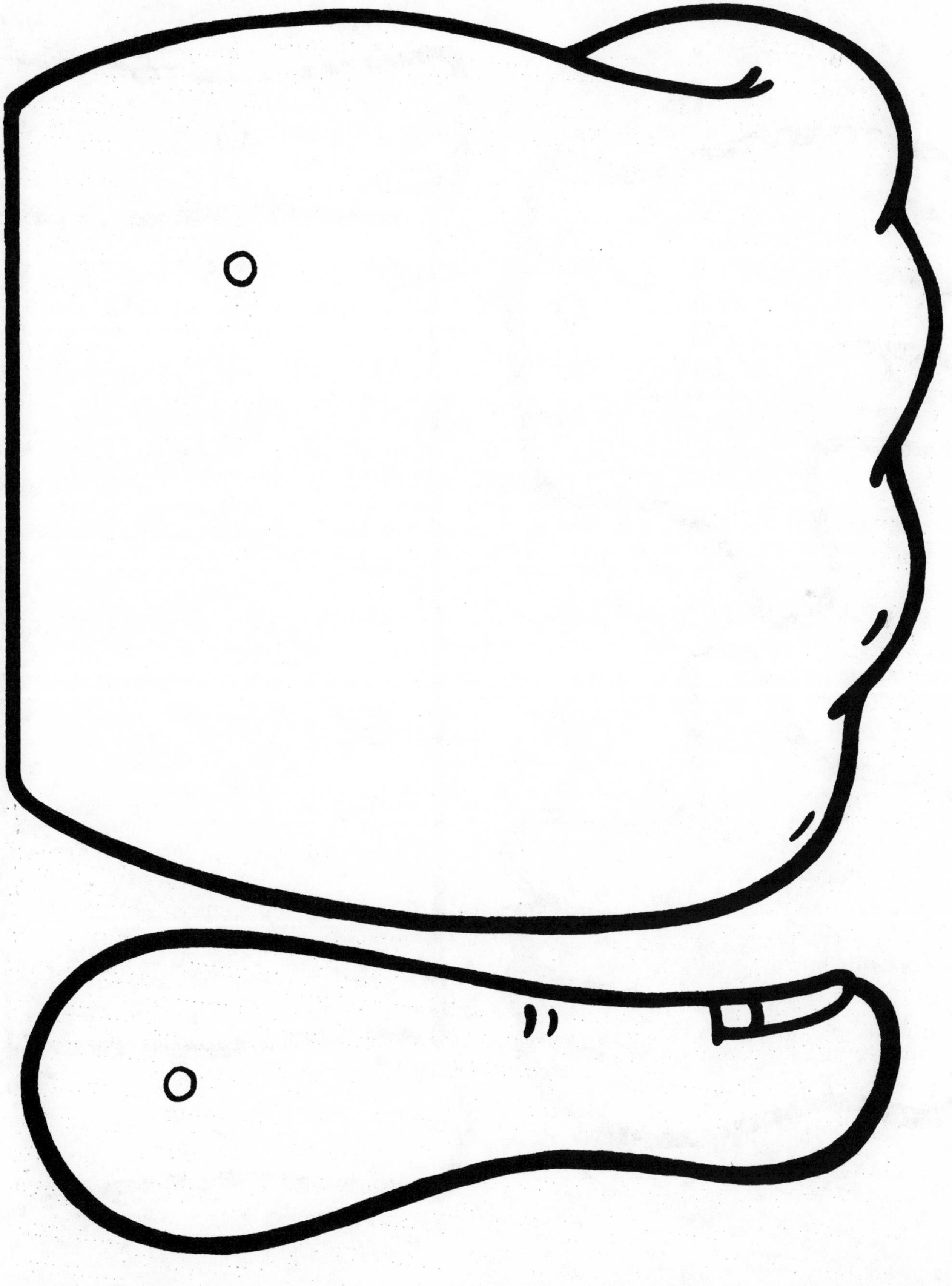

Thumbs Up! pattern

True-or-False Face

Materials

* Face pattern
* Plain-circle pattern
* Mouth pattern
* Scissors
* Construction paper and collage material
* Glue
* Paper fastener

TEACHING TIP

Use this tool for classroom management. If students are excessively noisy, show a frowning face. If students are quiet as they walk down the hall, show the smiling face. You might introduce a little game, where a high number of smiling faces means students will get a treat, such as a longer snack time.

Directions

1. Duplicate the face and mouth pattern (or use the plain circle pattern, so students can create original faces using collage materials).

2. Cut out the face and mouth.

3. Loosely attach mouth to face with paper fastener so that it can change positions.

Using the True-or-False Face

Use this learning manipulative to engage children in a discussion about character traits. Share a popular book series with your students (for example, *Fox* stories by James Marshall, *Franklin* by Paulette Bourgeois, *Nate the Great* by Marjorie Weinman Sharmat, *Amelia Bedelia* by Peggy Parish, and *Arthur* books by Marc Brown), and make statements about character traits that students should have noticed through the readings. Include statements that do not fit or apply to the character. Students will decide whether the statements are true or false, and will position the mouth on the face accordingly. Challenge students to support their positions verbally.

Other Suggested Uses

◆ **Language arts** Display an object, and give a list of descriptive words. For example, show a stuffed dog, and write the words pet, purple, and furry on the board. Students should indicate a true face if the descriptions apply, and a false face if they do not. For an extra challenge, include words that would elicit either response (for example, dogs are gentle—True Face/ False Face).

Instant Learning Manipulatives for Group Lessons   Scholastic Professional Books 2002

Head Band

Materials

* Head Band pattern
* Arrow pattern
* Crayons or markers
* Scissors
* Paper fasteners
* Stapler

★ TEACHING TIP ★

Because Head Bands can be easily flattened, they can be stored in an accessible bin for year-long use.

Directions

1. Duplicate the Head Band patterns.

2. Cut out the Head Band, additional strips, and arrow.

3. Color half of the band semi-circle one color, and the other half a different color.

4. Where indicated, attach the arrow to the semi-circle with a paper fastener.

5. Staple additional strips to the Head Band to adjust for length. Each student's Head Band size will vary, depending on head size.

Using the Head Band

Use this learning manipulative to support a variety of curriculum areas. Begin by assigning labels to each of the colors on the Head Band, depending on your area of study. For example, if you are studying the Amazon Rain Forest, one label could be plants and another could be animals. Students would move the arrow from label to label, depending on your discussion. Try using the Head Band in these other curricular areas: social studies—needs/wants, science—living/non-living, and language arts—true/false, fact/fiction.

Other Suggested Uses

◆ **Cooperative Group Work** Group members can create a three-colored Head Band to show you the progress and pacing of each group. One color indicates *We're thinking!*, another color indicates *We're working!*, and the third color indicates *We're finished!*

Head Band pattern

Puppet Person

Materials

* Puppet patterns
* Paper fasteners
* Scissors
* Crayons or markers
* Colored paper

Directions

1. Duplicate the puppet patterns on card stock.

2. Have students decorate the puppet with crayons, markers, or colored paper.

3. Cut out the pieces of the puppet.

4. Where indicated, attach arms to puppet body with paper fasteners.

5. On each puppet hand, denote the response cue that best suits your classroom needs: yes/no, or green dot (yes)/red dot (no).

Using the Puppet Person

When using manipulatives to teach awareness of the color, size, shape, and thickness of objects, encourage students to use their puppets, as well. As each manipulative piece is selected and placed in a classifying ring, students should use their puppet to show agreement/disagreement with the placement.

Other Suggested Uses

◆ **Social Studies** Conduct classroom voting using the Puppet People. Pick an issue, and let students decide how to show the opposing sides on the hands of the puppets. After the vote, students can tally the votes and discuss the outcome.

◆ **Math** During math problem solving, have students raise the puppet hand that reflects their agreement or disagreement with the solution.

◆ **Writing** Let students use their Puppet Person to indicate their genre choice during independent writing. Have students label the hands either fact/fiction, journal/article, or biography/interview. They then indicate their choice by positioning the hands.

Puppet Person pattern

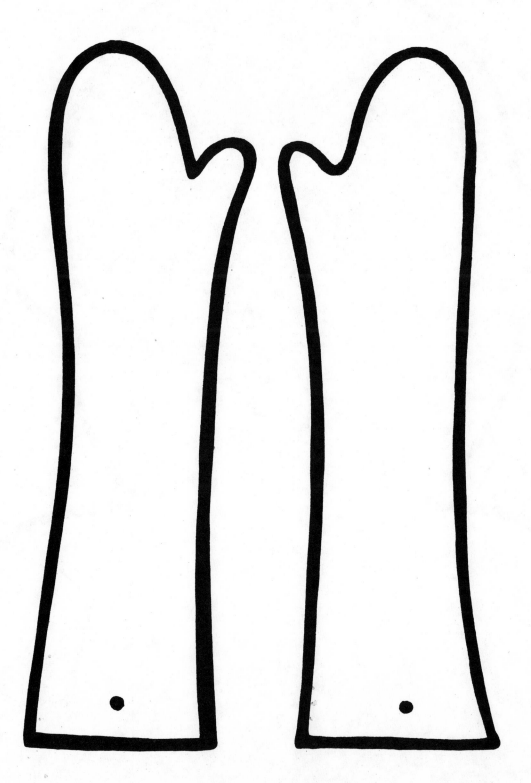

Instant Learning Manipulatives for Group Lessons   Scholastic Professional Books 2002

Puppet Person pattern

Fold Here

Bright Idea!

◆ Directions

1. Duplicate the light bulb patterns.

2. Cut out each light bulb.

3. Glue the wooden stick between the two light bulbs. This becomes the handle.

✳ Using Bright Idea!

Pick a story with a powerful ending, and read it aloud. Afterwards, discuss the ending. Then, invite students to create a new ending for the story. Allow students an appropriate length of time to think things through. While students are thinking, they display the *I'm Thinking* side of the light bulb. As they develop ideas they switch the light bulb to the *I've Got It!* side. This tool clearly indicates who is prepared to respond.

✳ Other Suggested Uses

◆ **Classroom Management** Use this tool during small group assignments. Pick a signal that means you are asking for the group's progress at a given moment. When you make the signal, a group representative holds up the light bulb, showing the side that best indicates the stage of progress. This tool will help discourage students from calling out *We're done!*

◆ **Math** Encourage students to use this tool as they figure out the answers to word problems or arithmetic questions.

◆ **Language Arts** As you explore stories with detailed plots or problems to solve, have students use their Bright Idea! tool to show what they have figured out, or what new twist they have discovered.

✦ Materials

* Light bulb patterns
* Wooden craft sticks
* Glue
* Scissors

✱ TEACHING TIP ✱

For early learners or ESL students, color code the bottom portion of the light bulb red for *I'mThinking* and green for *I've Got It!*

Bright Ideal pattern

I'm Thinking

I've Got it!

Thought Tube

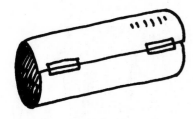

Materials

* Thought Tube pattern
* Strips of red and green construction paper
* Glue or scotch tape
* Crayons or markers

⋆ TEACHING TIP ⋆

Try using these other materials to make the Thought Tube:

* frozen juice containers
* paper towel rolls
* plastic tubing (can be purchased at a home improvement store)
* cut pieces of thick wood dowels
* empty film containers

Directions

1. Duplicate the Thought Tube pattern on card stock.

2. Glue a strip of red construction paper on one half of the pattern, and glue a strip of green construction paper on the other.

3. Cut out the pattern.

4. Create a cylinder shape by gluing or taping the edges together.

Using the Thought Tube

As students work on an assignment, they show their progress by standing the tube up on their desk. The red side facing you means the student is still working, while the green side facing you indicates that the student is finished and ready to move on. This is a handy way for you to learn which children complete their work quickly, while others take more time. Students might also use this tool to show agreement or disagreement with the ideas or opinions of fellow classmates.

Other Suggested Uses

◆ **Science** Assign more definitive labels to the different sides of the tube, such as heavier/lighter and hotter/colder. As you study and compare different life forms or objects, students can use their Thought Tube to show their predictions.

◆ **Classroom management** Students can signal the need for teacher support during an assignment by turning the Thought Tube red side up. Using the tool in this way will help to maintain a positive working environment.

Word Slide

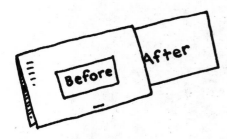

★ TEACHING TIP ★

Duplicate the blank word strip. Based on your classroom needs, you might label the two sides of the strip *right/left, yes/no, front/back,* or *happy face/sad face.*

Directions

1. Duplicate the Word Slide pattern.

2. Cut around the dotted rectangle to create an open window.

3. Fold the Word Slide frame on the dotted line.

4. Cut out the *before/after* word strip.

5. Insert the word strip between the Word Slide frame.

6. Staple the Word Slide frame on the open bottom edge.

Using the Word Slide

Use the Word Slide to play letter-order games, helpful for developing dictionary skills. For example, select one letter of the alphabet. If the letter *K* is chosen, ask if the letter *P* comes before or after the letter *K*. Students then use their Word Slides to respond to questions about letter order by sliding the words **before** or **after** into the open window.

Other Suggested Uses

◆ **Language Arts** Quiz students on the order of the days of the week and months of the year. The class then uses this tool to show which days and months come before and/or after each other.

◆ **Math** Review number order by using the Word Slide.

◆ **Social Studies** You might use this tool to review important concepts such as class birthdays, seasons, and applicable holidays around the year.

Word Slide pattern

After

Before

Instant Learning Manipulatives for Group Lessons   Scholastic Professional Books 2002

Punctuation Pyramid

✱ TEACHING TIP ✱

You might create and use blank pyramid forms as helpful management tools. For example, monitor work pace during independent activities by labeling the sides *My work is done*, *I need a teacher check*, and *My teacher has been here*. This will allow you a quick view of where each student is with his or her workload.

Directions

1. Duplicate the Punctuation Pyramid pattern.

2. Cut out the pattern around the solid line.

3. Fold on the dotted lines to create a pyramid shape.

4. Close the pyramid by taping the small folded flap behind the open panel.

Using the Punctuation Pyramid

Use this tool when teaching or reviewing punctuation skills. For example, write several sentences without punctuation on chart paper or chalk board. Have students read each sentence. Ask them to indicate which punctuation symbol is needed to end each sentence. Students respond by displaying the correct punctuation mark on the pyramid.

Other Suggested Uses

◆ **Reading** As you read a story aloud, students can supply missing punctuation. Pause when you reach the end of a sentence, so students know it is time to show the correct punctuation mark on their pyramids. Be sure to use your voice and facial expressions for emphasis, so students learn to recognize these important clues.

◆ **Classroom Management** Have students use this tool to let you know if they understand a new concept. Displaying the *?* means *I don't understand*, while displaying the *!* means *I understand completely*.

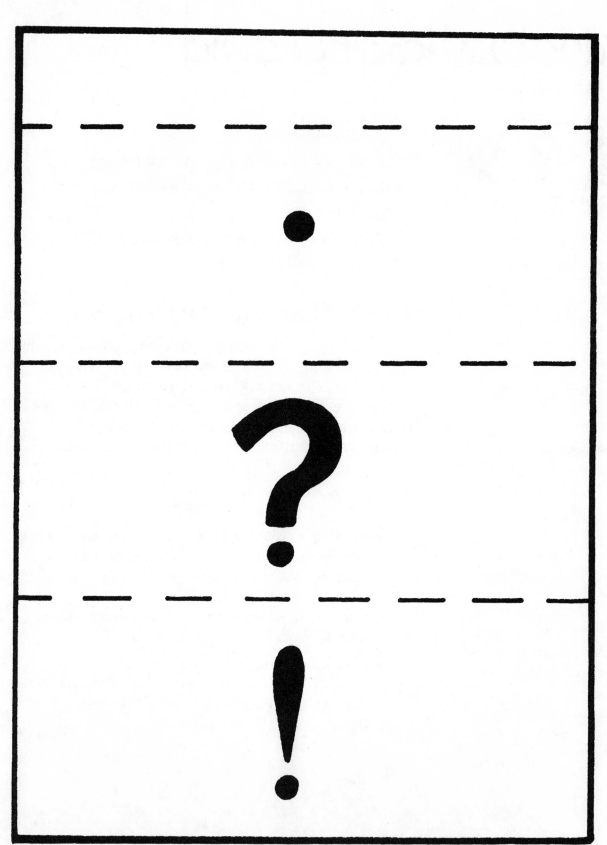

Dialogue Bubble

TEACHING TIP

Make a blank word wheel for customization. Encourage students to color their Dialogue Bubble.

Directions

1. Duplicate the Dialogue Bubble and word wheel patterns.

2. Cut out the window in the Dialogue Bubble.

3. Attach the word wheel behind the Dialogue Bubble using the paper fastener; the word wheel should turn freely.

4. Glue on the stick to create a handle.

Using the Dialogue Bubble

This is a helpful tool for evaluating data collected from tables and graphs. As you review these materials, ask students to make comparisons with the data. For example, if a table is comparing the weights of different farm animals, you might ask if the cow weighs more or less than the duck. Students would show their answer by turning the wheel until *more >* shows in the window.

Other Suggested Uses

◆ **Math** Use this tool for a variety of math lessons:

* The *more >* and *less <* responses, as well as the =, can be used during introductory lessons on inequalities.

* When sorting objects or numbers, students can use the *odd* and *even* responses on the wheel.

* For arithmetic and word problems, students can use the + and − responses to show their solutions.

Dialogue Bubble pattern

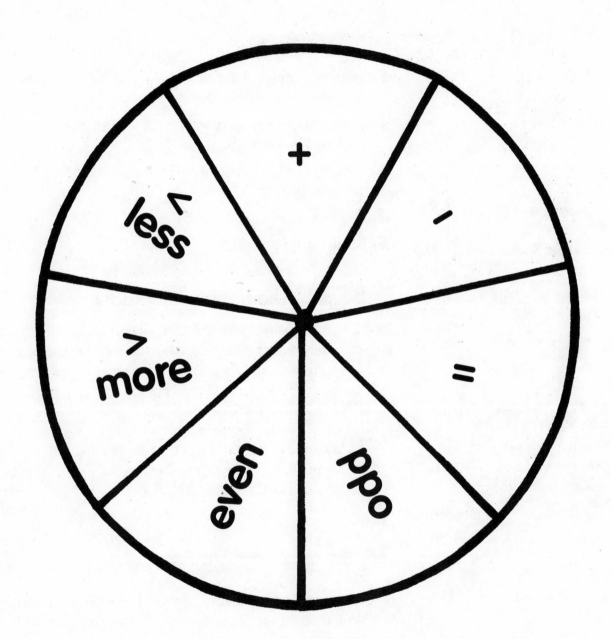

Number Spreader

Materials

* Number Spreader pattern
* Large paper fastener
* Hole puncher

★ TEACHING TIP ★

Store the Number Spreaders in plastic baggies to increase shelf life.

Directions

1. Make two copies of the pattern for each student, so they have the numbers 0–100.

2. Cut number cards apart and punch a hole on the spot indicated on each card.

3. Keeping two of each number together, stack the cards numerically from 0–9.

4. Slip a paper fastener through the stack.

5. Be sure that cards can be easily moved.

Using the Number Spreader

Play *Guess My Number* with this tool. Give clues leading to a chosen number. After each clue, have students display their answers with their spreaders. Discuss the range of answers before moving on to the next clue. For example, the chosen number is 32. Here are the clues:

>My number is less than 50.
>My number has a three in the tens place.
>My number is an even number less than 34.
>My number is higher than 30.
>Guess My Number!

Other Suggested Uses

◆ **Classroom Management** Use the Number Spreader during calendar activities. Count attendance, show the date, and even display the temperature!

0	1	2	3	4
.	.	.	.	.

5	6	7	8	9
.	.	.	.	.

Letter Spreader

Materials

* To create a single-color spreader, use the pattern for letters A–Z
* To create a two-color spreader, use the patterns for consonant letters and vowel letters
* Paper fasteners
* Hole puncher
* Scissors

TEACHING TIP

This is a great tool to use for games such as hangman. Instead of calling out letters, students can find letters in their spreaders and hold them up.

Directions

1. Duplicate the patterns. To make the two-color tool, reproduce the consonant letters on one color of card stock and the vowel letters on another color of card stock.

2. Cut the sections apart.

3. Punch a hole as indicated at the bottom of each letter section.

4. Arrange the letter sections in alphabetical order.

5. Insert the fastener through the section and secure so that the cards can be easily spread apart.

Using the Letter Spreader

It is important for early readers to recognize and manipulate word patterns. For example, begin instruction by identifying a rime, such as **ot**. Using this learning tool, students first isolate the letters necessary to show the rime. Then students provide an onset, such as **n**ot. As a class, a small group, or individually, students continue to extend the word pattern by manipulating the Letter Spreader. Individuals or groups can record the words found and create a class dictionary.

Other Suggested Uses

◆ **Spelling** Challenge students to a word hunt using the Letter Spreader. Working with this tool and a recording sheet, students search for two, three, or four letter words that can be made using only the letters on the spreader.

• n	• a
• o	• b
• p	• c
• q	• d
• r	• e
• s	• f
• t	• g
• u	• h
• v	• i
• w	• j
• x	• k
• y	• l
• z	• m

Letter Spreader pattern

a	a
e	e
i	i
o	o
u	u
y	y

b	n
c	p
d	q
f	r
g	s
h	t
j	v
i	w
k	x
m	y
	z

Vowel Cube

Materials

* Vowel Cube pattern
* Scissors
* Clear tape

★ TEACHING TIP ★

Use the Vowel Cube as a management tool. Have each student role the cube like dice. Then call all *a*'s or *y*'s to line up or transition to the next center, lesson, or activity. Continue until all kids have transitioned.

Directions

1. Duplicate the Vowel Cube pattern.

2. Cut along solid lines.

3. Fold along dotted lines.

4. Tape sides to create a cube shape.

Using the Response Cube

Use the Vowel Cube to strengthen vowel skills. For example, provide each student with a sheet of paper containing six labeled sections for the vowels *a*, *e*, *i*, *o*, *u*, and *y*. Students then roll the cube like dice, noting which vowel appears on top when the cube stops. Each student writes a word on his or her sheet that contains that vowel. Encourage students to refer to environmental print, the word wall, or dictionaries for assistance. The game continues until students have written five words under one of the vowels on the sheet.

Other Suggested Uses

◆ **Writing** Students can help you complete a story, thought, or quote of the day. On the board or overhead, create the piece of writing, leaving the vowels out of several key words. Then have students help you fill them in by displaying the correct side of their Vowel Cubes.

◆ **Reading** As you read stories aloud, stress certain words with vowel sounds. Ask students to show you which vowel you are sounding out by displaying it on the cube.

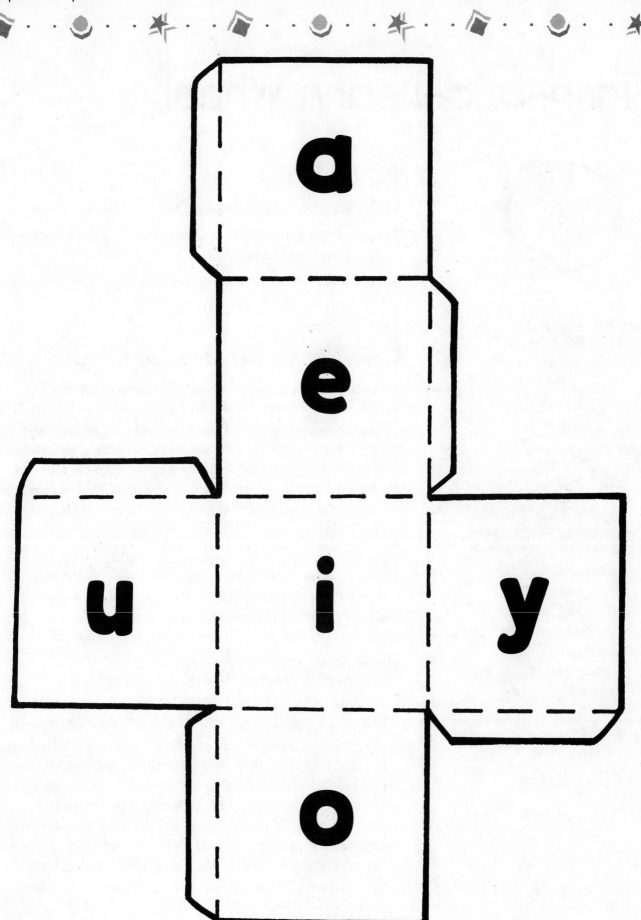

Turn-and-Learn Wheel

* Turn-and-Learn
  Wheel patterns
* Scissors
* Markers or crayons
* Paper fastener

Allow students to refer to real coins while they are working with the Turn-and-Learn Wheel. Handling these real props will help make working with money more meaningful and interesting.

Directions

1. Duplicate the pattern for wheel front and back.

2. Cut out the front and back wheel, and cut out the window along the dotted lines.

3. Attach front wheel to back wheel with paper fastener so that the back wheel turns easily.

Using the Turn-and-Learn Wheel

Students will have greater comfort with coins when they are familiar with the many features and details on each one. Use the Turn-and-Learn Wheel when reviewing coin features and counting. For example, after passing out the wheels, test students' knowledge about coins by instructing them to do the following: find the coin that shows the Lincoln Memorial, show a coin that has an animal on it, turn to the coin with flowers on it, and find a coin displaying the country's first president.

Follow the same procedure to practice counting with coins. Students can try the following: Show a coin worth 25¢, turn to a coin that is worth more that 5¢, find two coins that together equal 50¢, and find the coin that helps you count by 10s.

Other Suggested Uses

◆ **Reading** Make a blank wheel pattern to create a tool for reviewing story elements. In each section of the wheel, write one of the following headings: *Character*, *Setting*, *Problem*, and *Solution*. Pair up students and provide each pair with a wheel. Let students practice naming stories that fit the elements on the wheel. For example, one student in a pair turns to the element Setting. The other student must think of a story with a memorable setting, and then support it with evidence from the story. The students exchange roles and continue until each student has had the opportunity to match stories to each of the elements.

Turn-and-Learn Wheel pattern

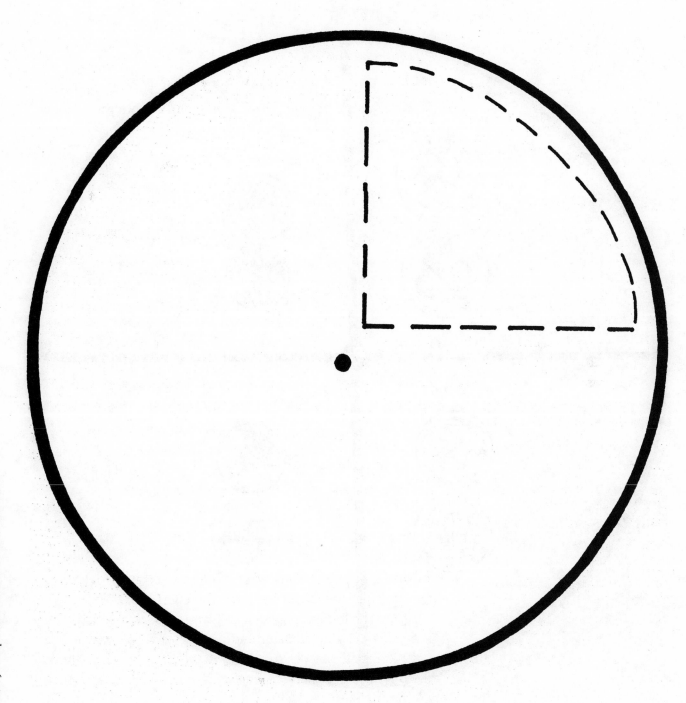

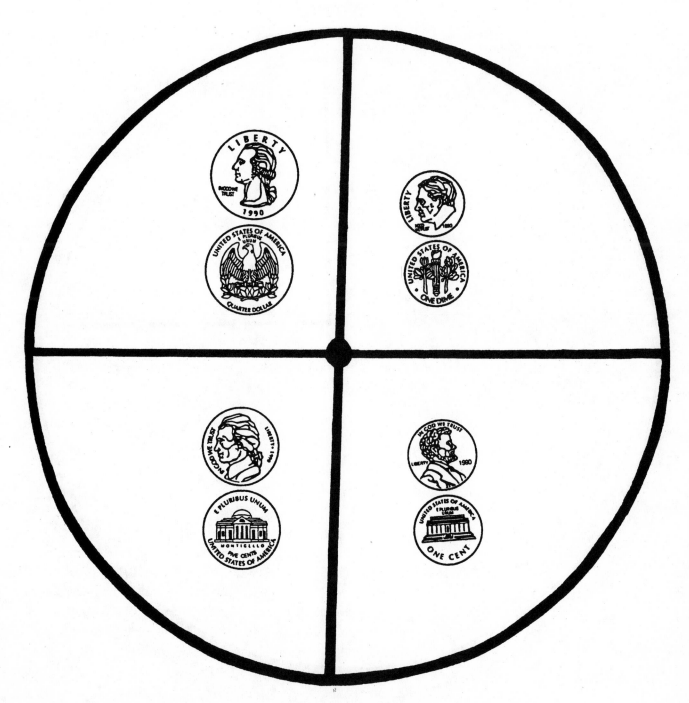

Instant Learning Manipulatives for Group Lessons Scholastic Professional Books 2002

Pick a Number

Directions

1. Duplicate the Pick a Number pattern on card stock.

2. Cut out the pattern.

3. Use crayons or markers to fill in the numbers.

Using Pick a Number

Use Pick a Number to do a quick vocabulary activity. On a chalkboard or chart paper, write and number four words from your classroom word wall to use in a game of *Guess My Word*. For example, you might write the following: *1. dog*; *2. cat*; *3. bird*; and *4. horse*. Secretly select one of the four words as the mystery word, perhaps *bird*. Students should gather with their Pick a Number board, a clip or pin attached to each numbered section. As you give clues about the mystery word, students detach the clips or pins from the numbered spaces that don't fit the clues. One clue might be that this word is an animal that can live in a person's house. The word *horse* does not fit this clue, so students remove the clip or pin attached to section 4. Continue until the mystery word has been discovered.

Other Suggested Uses

♦ **Classroom management** You can randomly arrange a class into two, three, or four groups using the Pick a Number board. To make two groups, attach one clip to half of the boards, and two clips to the other half. Then arbitrarily distribute the boards to the students, and have them break into two groups based on the number of clips attached to their boards. Follow the same procedure to form three groups or four groups. This helps to eliminate peer pressure in group selection.

♦ **Science** Write the following animal classifications on a Pick a Number board: *1. insects*; *2. amphibians*; *3. reptiles*; and *4. mammals*. As you call out an animal name, students place a clip or pin on the correct classification.

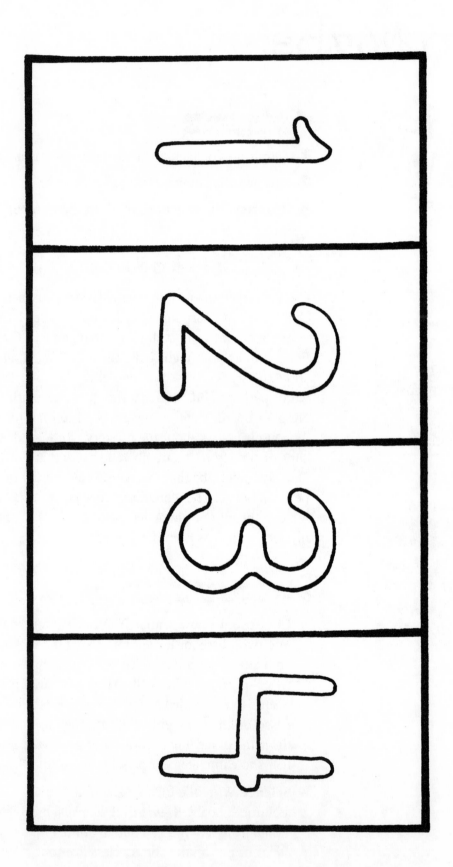

Compass

Materials

* Compass pattern
* Compass-needle pattern
* Paper fastener
* Scissors
* Crayons or markers

★ TEACHING TIP ★

To extend the concept of directionality, have students locate and label intermediate directions including northeast, southeast, northwest, and southwest.

Directions

1. Duplicate the Compass and compass-needle patterns.

2. Cut out the Compass and compass-needle.

3. Have students color the Compass headings.

4. Use a paper fastener to attach the needle to the Compass.

Using the Compass

Play a partner game called *Locate My State*. Each pair needs a labeled map of the United States, a small game marker, and the Compass tool. One student in the pair secretly thinks of a state. The other student tries to guess the state by placing a game marker on any state on the map and asking, "Is this your state?" If the answer is no, the first student must guide the second student to the secret state by indicating directions on the compass, one state at a time. After each move, the guesser tries to name the state. This activity provides an excellent review of names and placement of the fifty states.

Other Suggested Uses

◆ **Physical Education** Take students to an open area. Distribute a Compass to each one. Determine where north, south, east, and west are in that open area. Call upon a student to show the directions on his/her Compass. That student would then choose a movement for the class to follow in order to move towards the different directions (for example, hop, skip, crawl, or walk).

◆ **Writing** Assign spelling or vocabulary words to each letter on the Compass. Have students write them down on the wheel, and then play a game with a partner. One student spins and the other student must write a sentence using that word.

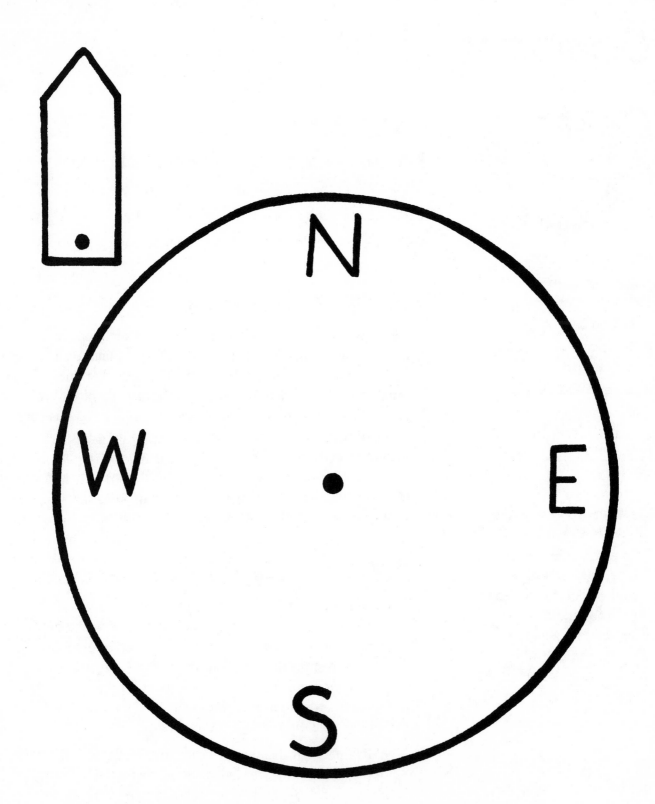

Behind the Door

Materials

* Behind the Door pattern
* Scissors
* Glue
* Colored beads

TEACHING TIP

This manipulative can be used interchangeably with Pick a Number (page 43).

Directions

1. Duplicate the pattern on regular bond paper so that the doors lay flat. Copy the pattern double-sided so that a number will appear under each door.

2. Cut out the pattern.

3. Fold on the solid line.

4. Cut on dotted lines.

5. Glue one bead on each door to create a doorknob.

Using Behind the Door

Use this manipulative to assess sequence skills after you've read a book aloud. Select a story and read it to the class. Afterwards, students should take out their Behind the Door manipulative. Explain that you will retell the story, out of order, and that they will use their tool to help you put the story events in the correct sequence. Explain that door #1 indicates the beginning of the story, door #2 indicates an event in the middle of the story, door #3 indicates another event in the middle of the story, and door #4 indicates the end of the story. Instruct students to open the door that corresponds to the part of the story you are retelling. For example, if you have finished reading *Charlotte's Web*, you might begin the retelling with, "Wilbur met Charlotte's babies." Students would open up door #4 as they realize that this event occurs at the end of the story. Continue your retelling until all of the doors have been opened.

Other Suggested Uses

◆ **Language Arts** As you dictate vocabulary words, have students open the door that reflects how many syllables they hear in each word.

◆ **Social Studies** Label door #1 *air*, door #2 *land*, and door #3 *water*. Students can categorize different vehicles, depending on where each vehicle travels.

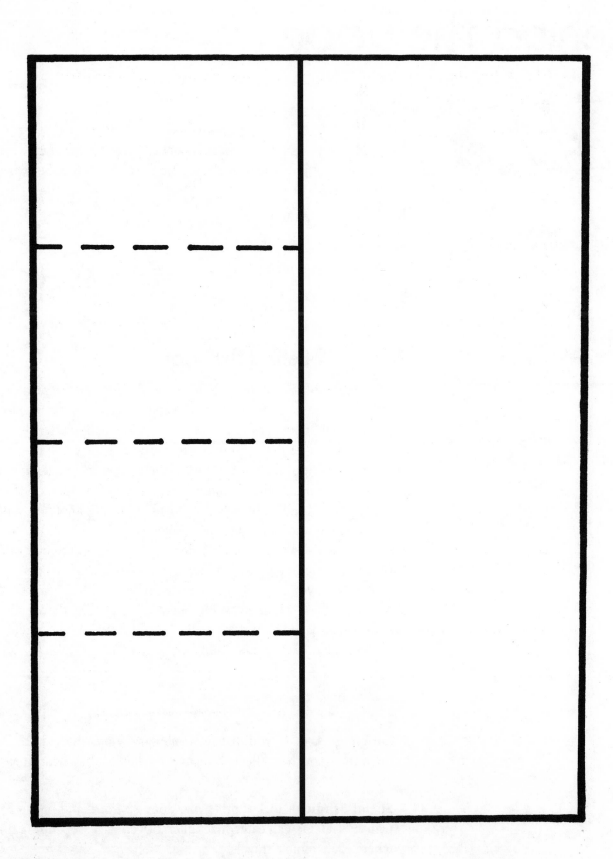

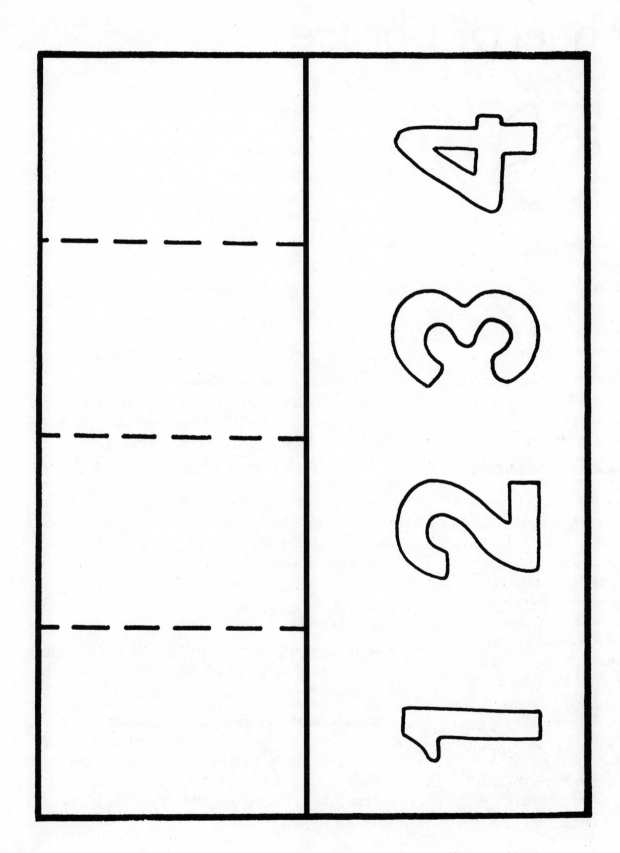

Wheel of Choice

Materials

* Wheel of Choice pattern
* Arrow indicator
* Paper fastener
* Crayons or markers
* Scissors

★ TEACHING TIP ★

Use the Wheel of Choice pattern to create other tools for your classroom curriculum. Duplicate the frame of the wheel and customize the inside to suit your needs. Separate the wheel into fifths to create a *five senses* tool, separate the wheel into fourths to create a *four seasons* tool, and separate the wheel into thirds for classifying scientific properties such as solid, liquid, and gas.

Directions

1. Duplicate the wheel pattern and cut it out.

2. Cut out the arrow pattern and attach it to the dot in the middle of the wheel, using the paper fastener. Be sure that the arrow moves freely.

3. Have the class select four colors to be used on the wheel, one color for each section.

4. Color the wheel the chosen colors.

Using the Wheel of Choice

Use the Wheel of Choice to explore the concept of probability. In this lesson, students will discover that a color can be always selected, sometimes selected, or never selected. Have students write the numbers 1–10 on a sheet of paper. Then have them spin the arrow, each time recording the color the arrow stops on. After students have finished all ten spins, discuss the results. For future probability activities, have students predict the outcomes ahead of time, and then revisit these predictions after completing the activity.

Other Suggested Uses

◆ **Math** Assign a number value to each of the four sections on the wheel. Have students spin the arrow a given number of times and then total the results.

◆ **Classroom Management** Let students help decide what they would like to do during free time. Label each section of the wheel with an activity, such as *silent reading, independent writing, recess,* or *a walk outside.* Then have a volunteer spin the wheel to determine the activity.

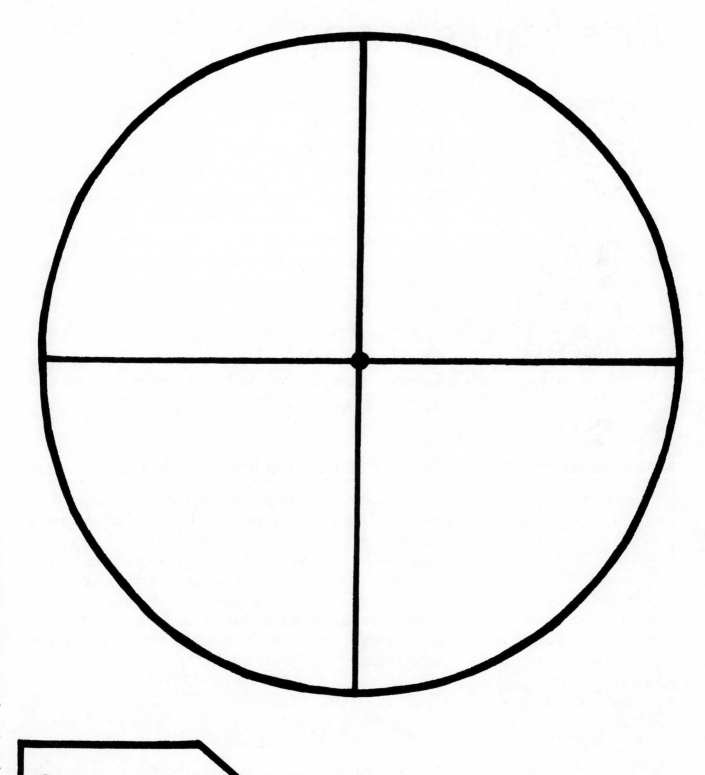

Time for Learning

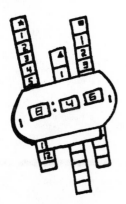

Materials

* Digital-clock and number-slides patterns
* Analog-clock and clock-hands patterns
* Paper fasteners
* Scissors
* Stapler

TEACHING TIP

Be sure to interchange clocks so that students become familiar with both formats.

Directions

For the digital clock:

1. Duplicate and cut out the digital clock and number slides.

2. Create space for the number slides by cutting on the dotted lines. Do not cut out the entire window.

3. Match the number-strip symbols with the symbols on each clock window. Thread the number strips through the windows of the clock.

4. Secure the front of the clock to the back of the clock by stapling the sides closed.

For the analog clock:

1. Duplicate and cut out the analog clock and clock hands.

2. Attach the hands to the clock using a paper fastener.

Using the Time for Learning Clocks

Use either clock format to give students a visual picture of time increments. Begin by having each student sit in a circle, holding a clock. Determine a beginning time and increment (for example: 12 o'clock—half hours), and display this on your clock. The student seated next in the circle then displays what the time would be a half an hour later (12:30). Continue around the circle as each student shows half-hour increments on his or her clock. For an extra challenge, have students work with unusual beginning times. For example, instead of starting with your clock on the hour or half hour, begin the activity showing 12:15 or 3:20.

Other Suggested Uses

◆ **Classroom Management** Assign one student each day to be the time keeper. When you announce the time and that students must get ready to switch activities, line up to go home, or go to a special, the time keeper must show the correct time on the clock.

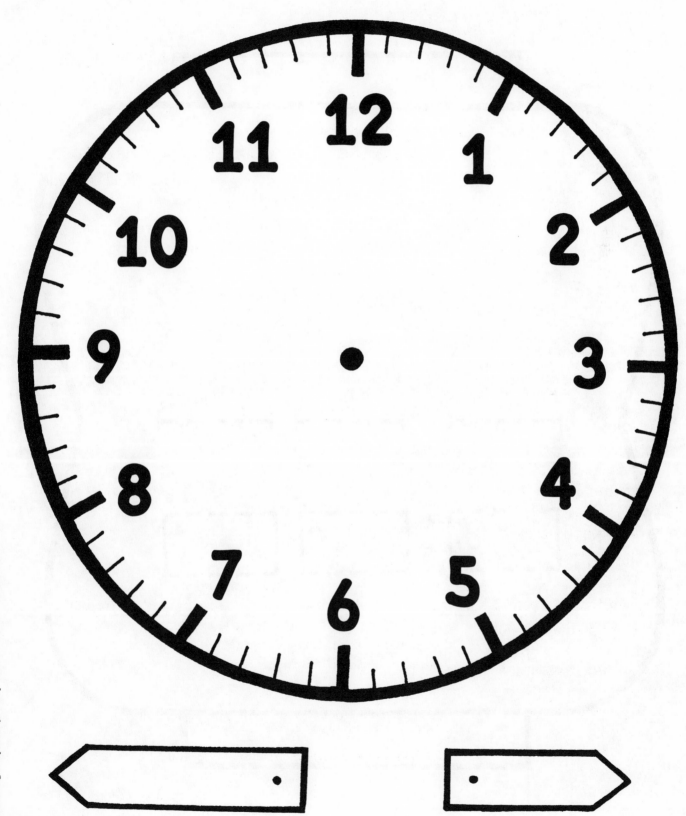

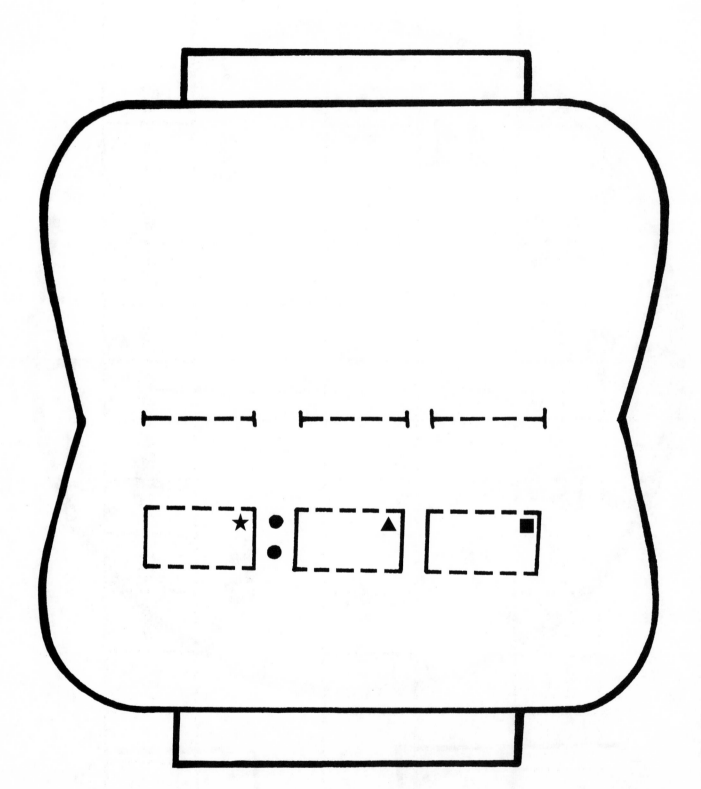

Instant Learning Manipulatives for Group Lessons Scholastic Professional Books 2002

★	▲	■
1	0	0
2	1	1
3	2	2
4	3	3
5	4	4
6	5	5
7		6
8		7
9		8
10		9
11		
12		

Finger Poke

★ TEACHING TIP ★

Watch to see how often the option *maybe* is selected. Make time for a discussion about risk-taking and the importance of comfort when making predictions, whether they turn out to be accurate or not.

Directions

1. Duplicate the Finger Poke pattern.

2. Cut out the pattern.

3. Cut out the circles on the dotted lines.

4. With a marker, outline both sides of each circle in the following order: top circle—green, middle circle—yellow, bottom circle—red. This assures that you, as well as the student, can view each response.

Using the Finger Poke

In this lesson, each student uses the Finger Poke to help interview a classmate. Practice the technique to ensure that students understand how to use the tool. Instruct the class that putting their index fingers through each circle indicates a different response to a question: green indicates *yes*, yellow indicates *maybe*, and red indicates *no*. Begin by modeling some questions that can be answered with *yes, no,* or *maybe* such as *Do you like to read? Do you like winter? Are you good at sports? Is spaghetti your favorite food?* Have students pair up. One student asks the questions and the other indicates the answers using the Finger Poke. Then partners reverse roles and begin again. Follow up with a class meeting to discuss the interview results.

Other Suggested Uses

◆ **Science** Encourage participation in a lesson featuring the concepts of *sink* and *float*. Before testing each object, have students make predictions using their Finger Pokes.

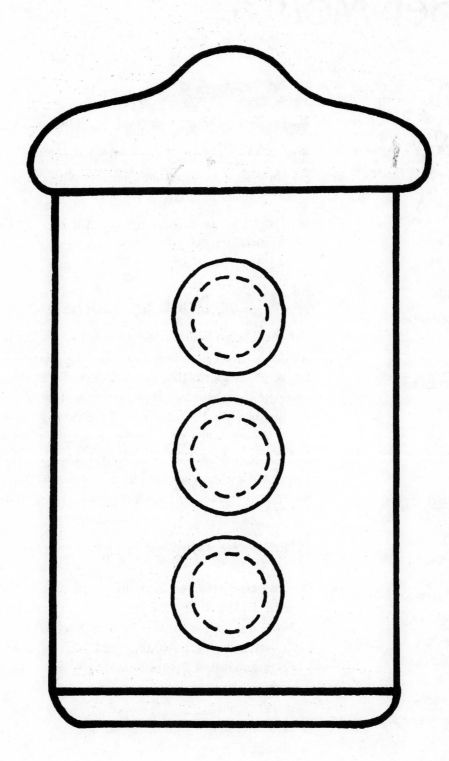

Instant Learning Manipulatives for Group Lessons   Scholastic Professional Books 2002

Blabber Mouth

* Blabber Mouth face and word-slide patterns
* Scissors
* Markers or crayons
* Collage materials
* Glue

★ TEACHING TIP ★

The word-slide format can be used to review any concepts that are part of a list. For example, planets, months, days of the week, or seasons can be added to the slide. This is a handy way for students to respond to your queries during lessons, or quiz each other for review.

▷ Directions

1. Duplicate and cut out the face and word slide.

2. Cut out face openings along the dotted lines.

3. Have students decorate the faces with crayons, markers, or collage materials.

4. Thread the word slide through the holes in the mouth, so it moves easily.

✹ Using Blabber Mouth

Use the labeled Blabber Mouth word slide during reading comprehension exercises. Read aloud a piece of literature. Explain to students that you will reread phrases or sentences from the story. After each phrase or sentence, students will use Blabber Mouth to indicate if the passage identifies *Who, What, Where, When,* or *Why.* For example, if the story is *Little Red Riding Hood,* students might indicate the following: a little girl wearing a red cape and hood = *who,* deep in the forest = *where,* and a basket filled with goodies for grandma = *what.*

★ Other Suggested Uses

◆ **Language arts** Use the blank word slide to list frequently used word endings such as *-s, -ed, -er, -est, -ly,* and *-ing.* Write a sentence containing a highlighted base word. Students should move the word slide to show the word ending that best fits the sentence. Discuss the possibility of more than one correct answer. For example, in the sentence *She _____ games. (play),* students could choose either the *-ed* or *-s* ending.

Blabber Mouth pattern

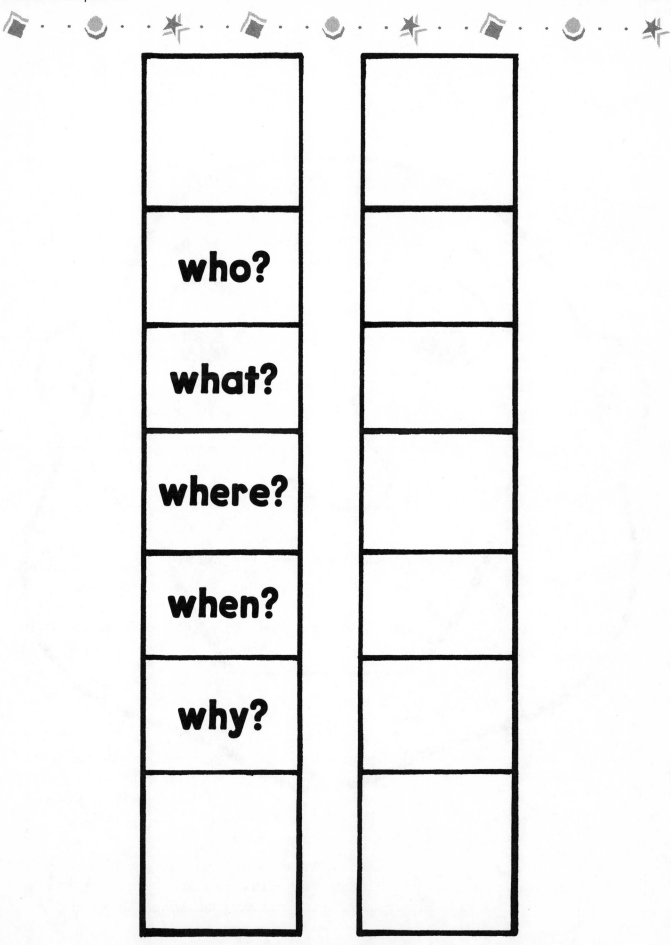

who?

what?

where?

when?

why?

Instant Learning Manipulatives for Group Lessons   Scholastic Professional Books 2002

Opinion Meter

Materials

* Opinion Meter patterns
* Clear tape
* Scissors

TEACHING TIP

Use this tool to allow students to express opinions about everyday occurrences, such as the weather, what they have for lunch, and their after-school activities. Remind students that we should respect the opinions of others, even if they differ from our own.

Directions

1. Duplicate the patterns for each student.

2. Cut around the outside of the meter and around the dotted rectangular window on the front panel.

3. Fold the meter on the dotted line. Close the meter with tape at the open edge, below the numbers.

4. Cut out the meter strip and slide it inside the meter, arrow end first. The strip should slide smoothly back and forth.

Using the Opinion Meter

Instruct students to use the Opinion Meter by sliding the arrow strip back and forth. If the entire black part of the arrow strip is showing inside the window, this indicates a high opinion. If there is some white showing in the window, this indicates a lower opinion. If there is only white showing, this indicates a very low opinion. Read a book to a small group or to the entire class. During or after the story, students can express their opinions about a selected aspect of the book. For example, perhaps you wanted to focus on a study of characterization. Students can react to the following questions, and show their opinions on their Opinion Meters: *How would you rate the main character's bravery? What do you think about the choices the main character makes?*

Other Suggested Uses

◆ **Assessment** Upon completion of a classroom activity such as cooking or art, have students indicate the success of the activity on their Opinion Meter. You might use this information to determine whether an activity should be repeated, adjusted, or replaced altogether.

◆ **Classroom Management** After working on a cooperative activity, group members can use their Opinion Meters to assess the dynamics and/or productivity of the group.

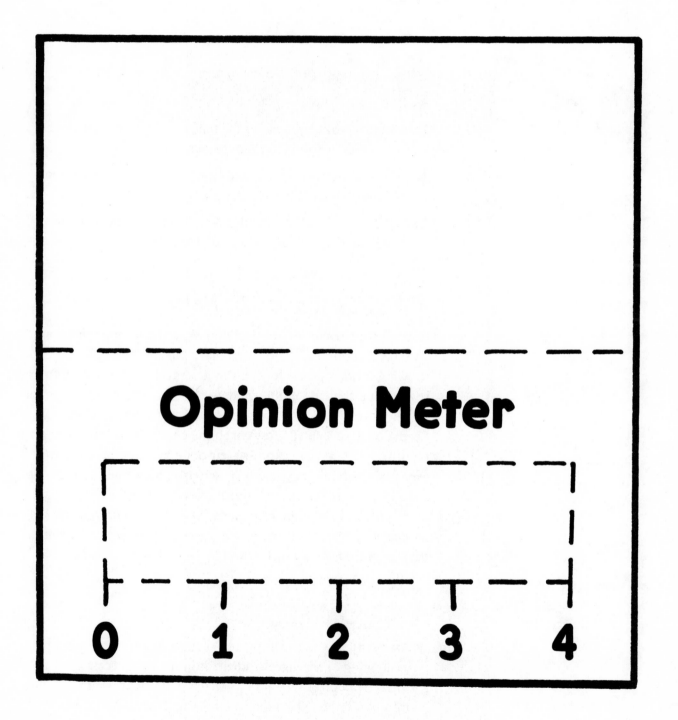

Opinion Meter

0   1   2   3   4

Instant Learning Manipulatives for Group Lessons   Scholastic Professional Books 2002

Notes